The Green Millionaire

The Green Millionaire

Monetizing Green Strategies In Emerging Markets

PATRICK GREEN

iUniverse, Inc.
Bloomington

The Green Millionaire
Monetizing Green Strategies In Emerging Markets

iUniverse books may be ordered through booksellers or by contacting:

iUniverse
1663 Liberty Drive
Bloomington, IN 47403
www.iuniverse.com
1-800-Authors (1-800-288-4677)

ISBN: 978-1-4697-9812-7 (sc)
ISBN: 978-1-4697-9813-4 (ebk)

Printed in the United States of America

iUniverse rev. date: 03/24/2012

And God said, "Let us make man in our image, after our likeness: and let them have dominion over the fish of the sea and over the fowl of the air, and over the cattle, and over all the earth, and over every creeping thing that creeps upon the earth"

Gen 1:26. King James 2000 Bible

DEDICATION

"It is not the critic who counts; not the man who points out how the strong man stumbles, or where the doer of deeds could have done them better. The credit belongs to the man who is actually in the arena, whose face is marred by dust and sweat and blood, who strives valiantly; who errs and comes short again and again; because there is not effort without error and shortcomings; but who does actually strive to do the deed; who knows the great enthusiasm, the great devotion, who spends himself in a worthy cause, who at the best knows in the end the triumph of high achievement and who at the worst, if he fails, at least he fails while daring greatly. So that his place shall never be with those cold and timid souls who know neither victory nor defeat."

—Teddy Roosevelt, April 23, 1910

I dedicate this book to all the people that gets to read it. Those that strive to excel and make a sustainable living with the consideration of nature in mind.

CONTENTS

Making money with conceptualized strategies will ever be in practice, the functionality lies in emerging markets at which inter-phase is strategy and innovation.

Everything starts with an idea. It is a choice to live a greener life. Sustainability dictates a selflessness that will make life more meaningful.

There is no need to reinvent the wheel but you can remodel it to suit your purpose.

INTRODUCTION

The driving force behind 21st century business is primarily the imagination of an entrepreneur. There are various tools that are applicable for finding innovative solutions to business problems; Technology is just one of them. The dynamics of new markets has an inter-phase that embraces innovation strategy.

Monetizing green strategies in emerging markets will enhance individual and organizational capabilities for innovation, and the strategic management of new technologies will ensure that an enterprise is built.

The book provides a detailed understanding of enterprise and value creation as captured in the 21st century, focusing on the critical role of emerging technologies and markets.

Readers will develop the skills required to analyze the value of new developments and opportunities, and the adaptation necessary for changing or fluctuating business environment.

The book explores the strategies that can leverage and sustain innovation, and the tools that can make it possible to create, deliver and capture value.

The definition of the strategic direction and scope to gain competitive advantage within the emerging markets by building and sustaining an enterprise through a sustainability focus is a key undertone throughout the book.

There is money to be made within the environmental sector, as well as in green businesses. It is the imagination and the ability of the entrepreneur to conceptualize a strategy, that will enhance the functionality of the money making process through enterprise.

The book practically shows the viability of money making green projects and the merging of environmental performance with the profit margin.

QUOTES

1. You do not need money to make money; the quality of your relationship will make you some
2. You can be environmentally compliant and still increase your profit margin; the solution is to know how to achieve the art
3. I know a man who made millions of dollars out of managing faeces, guess what, the money did not smell.

PART 1

MONETIZING GREEN STRATEGIES IN EMERGING MARKETS

The basic elements of the physical environment

The basic elements of physical environment are the following:

1. Land
2. Air
3. Water

The natural environments have living and non-living things within it, occurring naturally on earth.

Natural resources and natural systems like complete ecological units are the components of the natural environment.

There is a symbolic attachment to the colour green in nature. In nature the prevalent colour is Green and it has been ascribed to the following:

- fertility
- life

The colour green is in the world view of human beings. It is pleasing to the eye, the colour green is restful and pleasing. It gives a form of equilibrium; it is the colour of balance.

Green also means:

- growth,
- peaceful
- learning.

Green is considered to be a safe colour; it is the colour of choice when people are not sure what colour to use anywhere because it can create a background blend for all other colours.

The people that are well balanced in life favour the use of Green.

Green symbolizes the following:

- The master healer and life force
- Money
- Healing for the eyes

The people of Egypt of old use green eyeliner and this in itself depicts the ancient beautification tendencies. This use of the colour green is almost as old as history itself. Green eyeshades are still used by a lot of people around the world.

It has always been a good advice to eat vegetable or raw green foods for good health and good lifestyle in order to encourage greener living and its benefit for individuals as well as the environment.

GREEN ENERGY

Green contains the following:

- Powerful energy of nature
- Growth
- Desire to enlarge territories
- Desire to expand or increase
- Balance and sense of order

Change is a constant thing that is necessary for growth, and so this ability to sustain changes is also a part of the energy of green.

There are many way to generate green energy or energy for vitality. People that embrace nature or the environment and wants a state of equilibrium in their life should put some green in their life. This will ensure success in the pursuant of new ideas or in the development of new concepts.

Readers should therefore appreciate nature and green to be able to:

- Develop a fresh perspective on balance
- Experience growth in a new dimension
- Be free to explore in nature and life.
- Develop confidence and get protection from worries associated with persistent demands on their resources.
- Live a more sustainable life
- Develop the ability to meet present needs.

MEANING OF THE COLOUR GREEN

Green is a prominent colour in the rainbow and occupies more space in the spectrum visible to the human eye. It is second only to blue as a favorite colour. Green exists in or spread throughout the natural world and is an ideal backdrop in interior design because it is in our world view and a colour that we easily identify with.

There is a tranquility and refreshment in natural green, with a natural equilibrium of cool and warm (blue and yellow) undertones. Green is considered the colour of harmony and environmental systems.

The colour green has an impact on our psychological balance and this could be experienced in the following ways:

- Therapeutic in a soothing way.
- Psychologically and physiologically relaxing.
- There is alleviation and lifting of moods
- There is peace, freshness and harmony

Readers will get the best out of this book if they keep an open mind. My intent is to help readers, either individuals, corporate or public sector representatives to be able to make money by using nature, fertility, life, and learning and growth strategies in emerging markets in a sustainable manner.

To be able to harness the powerful energy of nature for growth or increase therefore, we must keep our mind on the symbolic use of green. There is an urgent need for change from polluting the earth to enable the transformation that is necessary for sustainable growth.

I will start by introducing you to Green Concepts Associates Limited. The organisation is a company limited by shares in the United Kingdom and is set up to ensure that all readers of this book or any of our other products have access to information and consultancy on green strategies and projects in emerging markets. The primary vision of the organisation is to equip the world for sustainability.

Green Concepts Associates Limited offers excellent integrated solutions, which are useful in enhancing green functionality, maximizing profits for clients by forming a synergy between environmental performance and the profit margin.

The strategy and innovation at the inter-phase of any emerging market is what we create and harness for the benefit of our customers. We enable private and public sectors to be competitive by conceptualizing a strategy that will enhance their functionality, through the anticipation of changes.

We empower individuals to be able to invest in new green technologies, waste to energy or marketable products that are generated by varied projects and also make a success of building a thriving business of choice.

Let us start by gaining more understanding of some of the key words in the body of the title within the context of this book.

> Monetizing: To monetize.
> Monetize: To convert into money.
> Strategy: This refers to a plan of action either short or long term that as being designed to meet certain objectives or achieve a particular goal.

Strategy is concerned with the long term success of the organisation as a whole, defining its direction and scope to gain competitive advantage (University of Oxford, 2009).

Emerging Markets are nations with social or business activity in the process of rapid growth and industrialisation.

I saw a green, wet luscious field and a sparse, discoloured and dry one side by side many years ago, at a very young age. The contrast, the differences and significance made me to realise the importance of caring for the environment, as well as catching a glimpse of the relevance of sustainability while thinking long term about the implication of drought.

My primary goal in life is to care for the environment and equip people to live a sustainable life. The interactions of individuals and companies (private or public sector) with the environment generate a huge amount of waste and pollution. The abuse of the environment is palpable. The degradation of the environment is widespread. All hands must be on deck to make a change. There is never a better time to make money while caring for the environment than now because there is a demand for information and knowledge on how to manage waste. The skills and applicable technology needed to be able to achieve this laudable aim are the foundation of this book.

Green Concepts Associates Limited will develop ideas of thoughts before and after it has been processed to enhance the functionality of conceptualised strategies, as well as individual and corporate perception and ability in building a good relationship with the environment by turning waste into useful products that can be marketed to generate alternative stream of income.

The issue of sustainability becomes a focus. The ability of the present generation to meet their needs without hindering the ability of future generation to meet their own needs is crucial. Deep considerations and effective planning is needed to be able to achieve this. The morality behind environmental care is intrinsic and the ramification is far reaching.

The ability to make money with green ideas and concepts by harnessing the huge biodiversity of the environment, as well as turning the waste generated into marketable products will ensure that.

To make money with green strategies therefore the focus should be the end products. I will talk about three waste management processes that are discussed in detail as examples of viable projects within the context of money making ventures. Each project is an opportunity that will be deliberated on within the main window of opportunity and the end focus is to help interested individuals and companies to be able to monetize the end products of these projects.

1. MANUFACTURED AGGREGATES

Mineral wastes are generally inert and non hazardous but are by product of extraction and processing of aggregates. Examples are the following:

- Ashes
- Sludges

- Mineral processing residues (in the manufacture of construction products)

The processing technologies to manage mineral waste with an outcome that can generate alternative materials and other by products in the production of manufactured aggregates are vital in the use of waste materials for alternative products.

Traditional and/or alternative materials can be used to produce manufactured aggregates. They are mineral based materials that are processed using thermal or chemical means to produce a granular material suitable for incorporation into a variety of construction scenarios

Introduction

A wide variety of waste materials can therefore be turned into the aggregates that have been mentioned above. These have been produced for a long time from powder dust and clay.

The natural materials for aggregates are derived from the following in the UK:

1. Crushed Rocks
2. Sand
3. Gravel

There are new developments in science and technology that enables the use of thermal processing units to design and manufacture aggregates from different combination of resource materials, such as:

- bio-degradable materials left over
- refuse or rubbish
- industrial and by-product powder
- granular materials
- construction waste

The reason why this process is useful is the fact that some amount of waste in the waste stream can be diverted to manufacture commercially viable aggregates. Waste generation, recycling and disposal play a key role in the development of the disposal alternative that we have been talking about so far.

The manufactured aggregates have a lot of benefits derived from their characteristics. The application of the mixed aggregates in differing scenarios therefore has made it more appealing to an emerging market in the waste management sectors and could be used by both private and public sector organisations. The processing technology will allow the substitution of natural aggregates for manufactured ones at a more cost effective rate.

There is a potential opportunity to reduce the waste that is meant for the landfill significantly because waste could be used as resources for aggregate manufacture.

The other benefits of manufactured aggregates are the following:

- waste to landfill can be reduced
- new waste management techniques can be developed
- non-renewable resources can be conserved
- the natural environment can be better conserved
- the cost of construction can be significantly reduced
- the built environment can be made more environmentally friendly
- making use of waste in construction waste stream

The individual, private and public sector representatives should be thinking about the viability of enterprises that can make use of a waste to product equipments. The end products are commercially marketable.

There are many social, environmental and economic values attributed to the project above that could be developed in gaining a competitive advantage if there is a focus on monetizing an applicable waste management strategy. The question on the mind of the perceptive reader should be on how to monetize these products.

The first project case is a generic evaluation of the application of waste materials within a process. Other examples will be specific waste management schemes.

We will try and develop this further through the application of marketing strategies for the products as well as integration of products for processes that generate multiple products.

2. ANAEROBIC DIGESTERS

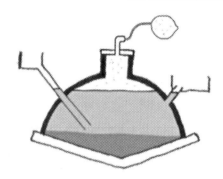

Figure 1
Small Scale anaerobic digester.
Source: Conradin, K., Kropac, M., Spuhler, D. (Eds.) (2010)

Executive Summary:

Small-scale biogas digesters Are reactors typically designed to produce biogas at the household or community level in rural areas, by the conversion of animal manure, Kitchen and garden wastes or toilet products into biogas. Biogas, is a mixture of methane (CH_4) and carbon dioxide (CO_2) and a nutrient rich sludge.

The airtight reactors are usually round underground chambers in which anaerobic digestion takes place during a couple of weeks up to several months, depending on a local temperature. It is filled with animal manure form the farm. Kitchen and garden wastes can also be added and toilets can directly be linked to the reactor for co-treatment of excreta. In the reactor, the anaerobic digestion transformers the organic matter into biogas, a mixture of methane and carbon dioxide, and a more or less stabilized sludge. The biogas can be used for cooking, heating or any other energy need. The biogas can be used for cooking, heating or any energy need. The remaining sludge-rich in nutrients—is a well-balanced soil amendment.

Table 1, illustrates the digester constituents.

In	Out
Blackwater, Faecal Sludge, Brownwater, Faeces, Excreta, Organic Solid Waste	*Biogas, Compost/Biosolids*

Source: Adapted from Conradin, K., Kropac, M., Spuhler, D. (Eds.) (2010).

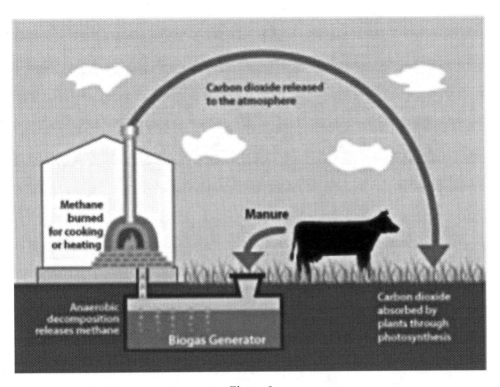

Figure 2
Overview flow chart of small-scale agricultural biogas reactors.
Source: State *Energy* Conservation Office SECO (*n*.y.) cited in Conradin, K., Kropac,
M., Spuhler, D. (Eds.) (2010).

The produced gas can be recovered and either directly for cooking and lighting or it can be transformed into heat in gas heater system or into combined heat and power (CHP) in a cogeneration unit (MES et al. 2003; JENSSEN *et al.*, 2004; WRAPAI 2009). The nutrient-rich sludge can be used as fertilising soil amendment in agriculture.

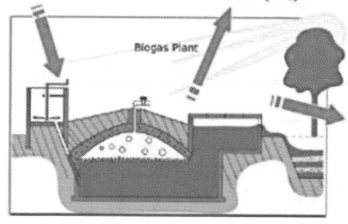

Figure 3
Overview flow chart of the effects
of small-scale agricultural <u>biogas</u> <u>reactors</u> to the environment.
Source: State <u>*Energy*</u> Conservation Office SECO (<u>*n*</u>.y.) cited in Conradin, K., Kropac,
M., Spuhler, D. (Eds.) (2010).

Checking the gas valve of a floating-dome biogas reactor in India
(left) and lighting the biogas flame (right, Lesotho, 2006).
Source: BIOTECH India (2007) and MUENCH (2008) cited in Conradin, K., Kropac,
M., Spuhler, D. (Eds.) (2010).

Table 2: Biogas guideline data

Suitable digesting *temperature*	20 to 35 °C
Retention time	40 to 100 days
Biogas energy	6kWh/m^3 = 0.61 L diesel fuel
Biogas generation	0.3-0.5 m^3 gas/m^3 digester volume per day
Human yields	0.02 m3/person per day
Cow yields	0.4 m^3/Kg dung
Gas requirement for cooking	0.3 to 0.9 m^3/person per day
Gas requirement for one lamp	0.1 to 0.15m^3/h

Source:. Adapted from WERNER et al., (1989); ISAT/GTZ (1999),
Vol. 1; MANG (2005) cited in Conradin, K., Kropac, M., Spuhler, D. (Eds.) (2010).

Animal manure and kitchen waste contain a lot of *organic* matter and generally, the process produces enough biogas for the family to cover at least cooking requirements. Humans produce *less excreta*, which contains less material that can be converted to biogas than animal dung (e.g. cows.) However, toilets, if available can directly be linked to the *biogas* plant where human *faeces* are digested together with the other wastes. This option provides a safe treatement of human excreta and thus improves the hygienic situation of the family. The availability of a renewable green *energy* sources reduces the use of firewood for cooking and indoor air pollution. Thus *biogas* digesters have the potential to minimise *health* risks and environmental pollution by using human *excreta* as a resources for providucing *energy* and *fertiliser* (GTZ 2007).

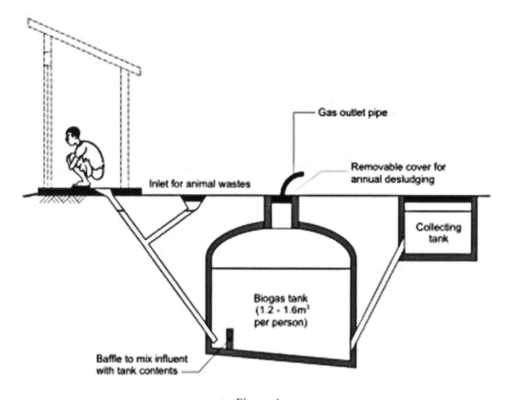

Figure 4
Typical small-scale biogas digester receiving animal waste.
Human toilet products are also added to the digesters allowing a safe treatment
and valorisation (e.g. toilet biogas plant).
Source: WELL (n.y.) cited in Conradin, K., Kropac, M., Spuhler, D. (Eds.) (2010).

Besides kitchen waste, garden wastes and plants can be added to the reactor to increase the *biogas* generation. Green plants are well suited for *anaerobic digestion* and their gas yields are high, usually above that of manure (WERNER et al. 1989). Or at least be pre-composted and preferably chopped before digestion (SASSE 1988).

3. COMPOSTERS

At Ridan Composting, we believe that sending food waste to landfill is wrong. It is unnecessary, unsustainable and costly! (Ridan Composters, 2009)

Our solution is an on-site **composter** for any catering facility that produces food waste. This includes schools, hotels, prisons and even climbing centres. (RIDAN COMPOSTERS, 2009)

Figure 5
A ridan Composter. Source: Ridan Composters, (2009)

Our in-vessel composter is simple and free to use, requires no power and is suitable for all food waste, including cooked and raw, meat and dairy. (RIDAN COMPOSTERS, 2009)

Our composter eliminates the need for catering waste disposal, not only saving money on disposal costs, but also saving emissions! (RIDAN COMPOSTERS, 2009)

Our composting equipment helps to recycle organic waste back into the environment; we help to raise awareness about the food cycle and food miles, especially in schools! (RIDAN COMPOSTERS, 2009)

Figure 6
Processed Compost by the Ridan Composter. Source: Ridan Composters, (2009).

The projects mentioned above produced products like rocks, water, biogas, digestates and compost. The rocks can be used for pavement works. The water can be treated and purified. The biogas is a renewable form of energy and can be used for cooking or fuel for cars. The digestates can be used as manure. They are not compost. The distinction between digestates and compost is that while compost is produced by aerobic digestion, digestates are produced by anaerobic digestion.

We must not forget that the book creates an opportunity to learn about the different enterprise building nuggets and teaches how to make money with the application of green strategies in emerging markets.

There are three crucial key performance criteria for the success of case-study work rate that will prove the feasibility of the above statement. This is the most important part of this book because it talks about the three key strategies that will make the reader a Green Millionaire.

1. The Window of Opportunity: Emerging Markets
2. The Integration of Products
3. Marketing: The automation of evergreen marketing sequences

The Green Business and the Environmental sector in the developing economies are dimensionally virgin. Any investment in this sector will thrive as long as there are skilled labour and expert designs in the implementation stage of the various projects. This book will empower new business start ups and start the process of equipping the world for sustainability. It will also enable business growth and development for those that have already started a similar project in any sector.

The tools and methodologies involved in building a viable, strong and feasible entity in Green businesses will be given to readers to ensure that they will be able to capitalise on this opportunity.

The conceptual analysis and application of green strategies will create a leeway for sustainable growth in the environmental sector. The increased functionality will create an amiable interest in things green and the people would have been empowered to take Mother Nature seriously.

The emerging market in this case scenario is the developing countries or nations. It is an open window of opportunity that must be tapped into.

The products that were generated by each project mentioned above or other products that are derived from individual waste to energy stream should be integrated. This will allow putting all the products, brand, service and programs together. This is a key product strategy that will enable the viability of any business case for the green projects mentioned above.

The marketing strategy must have a dynamic perspective and primarily sequential. There should be an automation twist to the marketing framework. This will enable capability of running it over and over again. The set of information involved in the build up must be evergreen. The tactics employed can vary but there must be a consistency in key points. Marketing is most effective as a streamlined, continuous process. It must be used to create new products in order to dominate an area.

The first green strategy I am going to talk about is an advice I will give to any budding entrepreneur, "always integrate". It is the strategy of integration—putting all products, brand, services and programmes together.

Starting, maintaining and sustaining any business could be systemised. Following a proven blueprint for business development and developing a passion for entrepreneurship will surely help.

If any business focuses on primarily building wealth without ethics, without values, with vision, stagnation will set in and that business will eventually crumble.

Harnessing resources and synchronic dominion of the environment without caring at the core of conceptualised strategy is a disaster waiting to happen.

The creative link between sustainability strategies in the present and the future is CARE for the Environment.

The necessity to create social, environmental and economic impacts for posterity sake, as well as focus on sustainability, has conferred upon my person, a goal, a purpose, a vision to be Green.

That eureka moment is not far flung when you expand your thoughts, disregard the mundane and embrace fresh perspectives.

The strategy and innovation at the inter-phase of the emerging market will synergise to ensure that there is a suite of integrated products whose functionality has been enhanced by conceptualised strategies within an open window of opportunity.

It is the intent of the author therefore to ensure that environmental performance is linked with the profit margin. The major improvements in environmental performance can be delivered through product design and innovation.

Let us quickly talk about another process of waste management before we summarise the use of the end products that have been generated in the initial projects that we have already talked about.

4. MUNICIPAL INCINERATORS

Figure 6:
Municipal waste incinerator. Source: Greenpeace, (2012).

Municipal waste incineration is still the number one dioxin source, according to a 1999 UNEP study. In many countries over the past few years, older incinerators have been updated and new incinerators have been built using improved technologies for air pollution control. This has led to substantial reduction of emissions of toxic substances to air

Figure 7
Municipal waste incinerator in Thailand. Source: Greenpeace, (2012).

Although this is an improvement, the problem of toxic waste products from incineration has not disappeared. In fact, the problem has shifted so that more dioxins and other toxic substances now appear in the ashes therefore creating new disposal and pollution problems.

Studies in Europe have reported that emission measurements from some European incinerators fall within the new proposed EC limit of 0.1 ng I-TEQ/m3, but others exceed this limit.

Industrial/Hazardous waste incineration

Only a few studies have been published in the scientific literature on recent emission testing of industrial incinerators.

Figure 8
Fiu-Swan Hills hazardous waste incinerator. Source: Greenpeace, (2012).

In Japan, a study performed point measurements on nine industrial waste incinerators (Yamamura et al. 1999). Dioxin emissions were below 0.1 ng I-TEQ/Nm3 for two of the incinerators and above this level (0.13 to 4.2 ng I-TEQ/Nm3) for the remaining six.

In the US, one study reported on dioxin emissions of mobile soil burning incinerators (Meeter et al. 1997). On-site remediation of contaminated soils at hazardous waste sites by such incinerators is employed where sites contain compounds that are difficult to destroy. Data collected primarily from trial burns of 16 incinerators showed that 10 of the incinerators failed to meet the proposed EPA standard of 0.2 ng TEQ /dscm. The authors commented that a significant fraction of soil burning incinerators could have problems meeting the proposed future EPA limit.

Medical Waste—useful waste into hazardous waste.

Only 10 percent or less of a typical hospital's waste stream is potentially infectious, and that can be sterilised with heat, microwaves and other non-burn disinfection technologies. The remaining waste is not infectious. Most paper, plastic food waste and other hospital waste are similar to the same waste coming from hotels, offices or restaurants, since hospitals serve all of these functions. By burning medical waste in an incinerator the basic biological problem of disinfecting infectious material—which can be dealt with by various technologies—becomes a formidable chemical pollution problem that is costly to manage and difficult to contain.

Waste to energy schemes

The generation of energy from waste has increased recently and in fact is used extensively by governments and industry to "green" incineration and make it more acceptable to the general public. But all of the negative impacts from incineration do also apply to "waste to energy" facilities. Moreover, the energy used to produce the product will get lost anyway and only a fraction of the intrinsic energy content of the materials will be recovered. Reuse and recycling are also from energy perspective preferred options.

Municipal solid waste can be directly combusted in waste-to-energy incinerators or it can be processed as refuse-derived fuel (RDF) before incineration (or combustion in e.g. powerplants); or it can be gasified using pyrolysis or thermal gasification techniques.

Another MSW-to-electricity technology, landfill gas recovery, permits electricity production from existing landfills via the natural degradation of MSW by anaerobic fermentation (digestion) into landfill gas. Anaerobic digestion can also be used on municipal sewage sludge.

Refuse-derived fuel (RDF)

Refuse-derived fuel (RDF) typically consists of pelletized or fluff MSW that remains after the removal of non-combustible materials such as ferrous materials, glass, grit, and other materials that are not combustible. The remaining material is then sold as RDF and used in dedicated RDF boilers or co-incinerated with coal or oil in a multi-fuel boiler.

The environmental concerns of incineration also apply to RDF combustion facilities.

Pyrolysis/Thermal Gasification

Pyrolysis and thermal gasification are related technologies. Pyrolysis is the thermal decomposition of organic material at elevated temperatures in the absence of gases such as air or oxygen. The process, which requires heat, produces a mixture of combustible gases (primarily methane, complex hydrocarbons, hydrogen and carbon monoxide), liquids and solid residues. Thermal gasification of MSW is different from pyrolysis in that the thermal decomposition takes place in the presence of a limited amount of oxygen or air. The produced gas that is generated can then be used in either boilers or cleaned up and used in combustion turbine/generators. Both of these technologies are in the development stage with a limited number of units in operation. Most of the environmental concerns for incineration also apply to pyrolysis and thermal gasification facilities.

Cement Kilns

Throughout the world some 60 cement kilns have been modified so that various wastes can be burned along with conventional fuels. But cement kilns are designed to make cement and not to dispose of waste. According to a study by the US Center for the Biology of Natural Systems, emissions of dioxins are eight times higher from cement kilns burning hazardous waste, than from those that do not burn it.

The above is an alternative method of waste management and is different from the initial projects that we have show cased. The process involves combustion of waste to energy. Some of the initial projects involve a biochemical process while the incineration project is thermal.

Public sector organisations might be interested to know that Green Concepts Associates Limited will facilitate the application of new technologies to ensure that the toxins generated are within a controlled environment and are adequately treated.

The products that we have discussed above are all environmentally friendly, innovative and are energy efficient. The strategic input cuts across products, marketing and the window of opportunity as detailed above. Production companies could be environmentally compliant without lowering their profit margin.

The strategies involved in associated products design, development and up till the point of marketing are relevant in any emerging market and should not be limited to green projects alone.

PROJECT MANAGEMENT

A project is a finite process that has a start, middle and end. In order to ensure that the projects mentioned above, as well as other projects are successful therefore, there must be a methodology or applicable tools to manage the projects.

There are key principles that should be observed by any project:

- There must be a brief that detailed the project objectives
- There must be a reason for the project
- There must be a plan to achieve project outcomes
- There must be detailed responsibilities and roles in the achievement so that the commitment to the project is genuine.
- There is an increased chance of success for well managed projects.

There is a demand for good project management in all sectors of the economy and the individual that want to invest in any project will be well disposed towards such an investment when assured of a higher percentage of success.

Change is the only constant thing. The business environment (private and public sector) organisations experience change for a number of reasons:

1. The nature of a business is to introduce new products, services and delivery mechanisms in order to stay competitive.
2. There are external influences (competitive pressures like legislation and policy) that causes changes in business processes, structure and culture

Change is inevitable and is often critical to survival in order to achieve greater efficiency and getting a better value for money.

There are inherent risks associated with change that must be managed effectively in order for the innovation and strategy mentioned above to deliver a successful project.

I have showcased a few projects above and think that it is important to bring to the world view of the readers how the effective use of conceptualised strategies, ideas, resources, skills and technology to achieve business objectives and deliver business benefits could be the primary criteria for building a successful enterprise.

A very good project management process will ensure that project risks are identified and managed appropriately, and objectives and benefits are achieved within budget, within time and to the required quality.

A standard method of project management with a flexible and adaptable approach must be in place to suit all project types. There are wide varieties of activities required within a project and the project management method should be able to provide a framework that covers these activities and disciplines.

The development of a business case that can justify the business and drive all the project management processes, from initial project set-up through to successful finish is a must.

In order to ensure that the project is successfully managed therefore, there are 22 evolving documents that will be produced for the client:

1. The business case
2. The project definition

3. The blueprint product description
4. The project brief
5. The project initiation document
6. The stakeholder map
7. The roles and responsibilities
8. The risk management strategy
9. The information management strategy
10. The benefit management strategy
11. The quality management strategy
12. The issue resolution strategy
13. The quality management plan
14. The benefit profile
15. The quality log
16. The risk log
17. The highlight report
18. The benefit realisation plan
19. The lessons report template
20. The lessons log template
21. The project quality plan
22. The end of project report

I will not explain the details of the content of the documents above because they will be developed for the clients that have a desire for their businesses to be successful. The documents above will help to ensure that the projects are well set up and managed for success.

Green Concepts Associates Limited will ensure that all projects are:

- well documented,
- managed by skilful labour and team,
- supported by the right technology to ensure that there is a higher percentage rate of success for investors.

I will now conclude this part with a write up about team dynamics and the application of effectiveness in team building. The excerpt below is a write up that I got permission to use from Susan Doherty at groupjazz:

TEN KEY ELEMENTS FOR TEAM LEADERS TO MANAGE

"There are other key elements that make a critical difference in how well the team is able to work together. Managing these ten dimensions can help make the team more effective.

1. PURPOSE
2. ROLES
3. CULTURE
4. CONVERSATION
5. FEEDBACK
6. PACE
7. ENTRY AND RE-ENTRY
8. WEAVING
9. PARTICIPATION
10. FLOW

These ten dimensions can be the beginning of a vocabulary the team can share to help support conversations about team process. These themes are interrelated so you can cover a lot of ground by choosing one or more as a conversation-starter and letting the dialogue develop naturally from there

PURPOSES

All the research on virtual and distributed teams shares the conclusion that having a clear, explicit, compelling, shared purpose around which everyone is aligned is the most important factor associated with team success. But for a distributed team, feeling purposeful requires more than agreement on the global purpose of the team. It's also important to have many small goals in addition to the larger overall purpose, which are achievable early in the team's existence. You can begin to build trust among team members via team-building exercises at an initial face-to-face meeting. However, trust really develops when team members count on each other for specific tasks. Therefore, it's important to create opportunities for team members to come through for each other early and often in the life of the team. Some short-term goals may fall naturally out of the work of the team. But many good candidates for these early exchanges can emerge from processes related to building the team and establishing working relationships. It's important for the tasks to be relevant and valuable rather than busy work, but they don't need to be difficult or time-consuming. For example, the team might decide to gather answers to a survey about a particular problem from the perspective of each country represented on the team and share those. You might decide on a common format for describing and sharing the experience, skills, and interests of individual team members for a collective resource bank. You might ask each team member to take on the task of exploring a particular communications option available to the team and work up a profile of it in terms of accessibility, team preferences, and where it might be used most effectively. Create a process where the team can decide together on one or more short-term projects so that they can share, succeed and celebrate as soon as possible. What are some candidates for tasks/projects for this team that can be delivered in a week? Two weeks? One month?

ROLES

In a distributed team it's easy to default to a pattern where everyone looks to the team leader to play all the needed roles because we lack the skills necessary to sort out who is going to play which roles when we're not in the same room. This makes the team weak and over-dependent on one person. When we're together face-to-face, it's easy for a group of people to look at each other and naturally work out who is going to do what. It's much harder in a distributed group to figure out where the gaps are, where a vacuum exists, where it's appropriate to step up and volunteer to take something on. We don't have the experience and skills to "feel out" the group and be comfortable with informal mechanisms to negotiate roles. In addition, roles are more complex in a distributed group because there are more roles needed and many of them are new and unfamiliar. Distributed teams may need technical support, knowledge archivists, and specialists in using different media. You might want to designate someone to notice when a team member hasn't been heard from in a while and follow up with them. The team could decide to take turns with the tasks of serving as liaison to other teams or functions. For both traditional and new team roles, virtual teams need to spend more time being explicit about mutual expectations for facilitators, managers, and members because the patterns of behaviour and dynamics of interactions are unfamiliar and it's easy to fall into misunderstandings and become frustrated with each other. What roles does our team need? How will we define these roles? How will we share the roles? What's our strategy for re-evaluating roles and players as we go along?

CULTURE

The culture of a team is influenced by the personalities of the members and the team leader, the environment in which they work, the nature of the communications media they use, the stories they have to tell about the team, their rituals and celebrations, and their shared language. Too often, distributed teams are missing many of the elements that are critical to developing culture because we haven't developed a repertoire of new strategies using the new media. How can we create celebrations virtually? How can we make sure we don't limit our communications to task-specific exchanges that leave out the all-important storytelling? Whichever combinations of media you are using to support a virtual team, you need to think through how these media will affect the culture of the team's environment. What metaphors are you using for interactions? How will these metaphors cue team members to think about where they are and what they're doing? An electronic space called "Project Database" will invite a different style of communication than one called "What's Happening Where You Are?" Keep in mind that you are creating an environment to support relationships, not just to exchange information. What norms, styles and behaviours would help or hinder the ambience and create the team culture you want? What adjectives do we want to associate with the culture of our team? (supportive, deep, fun, fast-moving, reflective, cutting-edge, information intensive, risky, intense, focused, creative,???). What do we need to do to create that culture? What strategies can we develop so that we can celebrate team success even when we're not together face-to-face? Where we will tell our stories.

CONVERSATION

One way to think about a team is as a network of conversations that cover a broad range of topics and questions: What will it take to meet our critical strategic goals? How the team's processes are working? How are individuals on the team doing? What's going on in the company? What's going on in the world? What are people on the team reading and thinking? What problems need attention? What should we be doing next? A team will function best if it feels like everyone is part of a continuous, daily conversation with the whole team. This doesn't happen unless you think about the design and facilitation of day-to-day interactions as well as special off site meetings and retreats. Typical meetings that rely on one-way communication don't engage participants adequately. Instead, draw on more "liberating structures" to allow the conversation to produce generative and innovative outcomes. Of course, in a distributed team, this is not achieved easily. A big danger for distributed teams is that their communications get stale and boring. When we're together face-to-face we create a lot of variation in our exchanges by meeting in different settings, using multi-media to spark discussion, and changing the style of meeting from presentation to dialogue. It's critical to keep the team communications fresh and growing—both qualitatively and quantitatively. At the same time, you need to watch for overload. Too many new messages overwhelm people. Assess the total volume of team communications daily and you'll see considerable variation from day to day. At the end of each week, ask yourself about the pace and the range of communications exchanged. Are the conversations still interesting, or have they become stale? What kinds of conversations are important for us to have regularly?

FEEDBACK

Since using technology as a primary means to communicate will be new to most team members, participants need to spend more time than usual talking about the quality of their communication. The team leader can provide some feedback but it's even better if participants develop a norm of providing feedback to each other about communication style, frequency, clarity, etc. It helps if team members can learn how to access more of their own feelings and reactions to messages in different media. One good strategy is to create a space within the communication system for the meta conversation about how everyone is feeling about their own and the team's use of different communications media. Any new unfamiliar medium can be problematic when we give feedback and the media associated with virtual teams is particularly difficult. Feedback meant as constructive could be misinterpreted easily when it lacks the facial expressions and other body language that communicates the spirit in which it is given. Give positive as well as negative feedback. Be direct but supportive. What norms can we create to feel safe when we give each other constructive feedback about our communications via new media? What strategies do we need to make sure we integrate and learn from what works and what doesn't for us in different media?

PACE

In distributed communications environments, PACE is an important dimension to facilitate. Different team members may access various parts of the team's communication systems more or less frequently. Some group members will sign on to get e-mail four times a day and some will let a whole week go by before signing on again. The term rolling present can be used to describe a phenomenon of distributed teams where the sense of team-time varies among the group. Generally, people consider material current if it has been entered since they last signed on. If you have several members who sign on four times a day, they may make it difficult for most group members to engage with the virtual group: it will all go by too fast. You may need to do some things to slow down the pace. Ideally, the team should establish norms for how often everyone will engage with the team. However, it will inevitably happen that differences in pace will develop. One way to even out the rolling present is to provide cues that let participants know what's important so that they can catch up easily, for example via e-mail updates that summarize the ongoing discussion. In addition to paying attention to the ongoing pace of the team's communication you also need to think about patterns of communication. A living system has a pulse. High performing teams operate as living systems. Collocated teams have natural mechanisms for creating this feeling—they're in the same time zone, have coffee together, say good-bye as they leave for the day. Distributed teams need to have a pulse too. One way to do this is to create cycles of activity so that team members start to feel the pattern—a weekly phone call, an online check-in item, and monthly celebrations. What kind of pace does this team need and want? (fast, slow, cyclical). How are we going to give our team a pulse so it feels alive?

ENTRY and RE-ENTRY

A fact of life of distributed teams is that members can seem to come and go because of many factors including travel schedules, local conditions that demand shifts in the individual's focus for periods of time, and cultural differences in calendars and holidays. In a face-to-face meeting it would be very disruptive to the flow of conversation to have people coming and going in the middle of the meeting. The quality of the exchange would not be as good if people were never sure of who was really participating and who was only peripherally involved. After a while it becomes difficult to remember who was "there" during a particular exchange and who only joined later. One of the advantages cited for virtual workgroups is that they are more flexible around time than face-to-face meetings. But it's still disconcerting when a group isn't sure of who is "there," what it means when they are not participating actively, and whether and when to expect their participation. You need to develop some strategies to handle the entries and re-entries of team members so that everyone knows when everyone else is there, when they are leaving, and when they are coming back. How are we going to announce our comings and going to the rest of the team? What strategies can we develop to help each other catch up when we've been away?

WEAVING

It's easy for a distributed team to feel disconnected. Their communications can seem disjointed, relationships can be fragmented, and connections to other teams and parts of the organization can seem fragile. The team needs strategies to weave the threads of their communication together, to weave themselves together as a network of relationships, and weave their work into the fabric of the larger organization. Weaving is a networking term that often refers to the process of summarizing and synthesizing multiple responses in a virtual group. The weaving item or response tells people where they've been, where they are, and where they might want to go next. It can identify issues people agree on or issues that still bring up many questions or require more information. Weaving can also link what's going on in one part of the communication system with another. Weaving gives all members, however long they've been participating, a chance to start fresh or take off in a new direction. It can help keep the group from spinning its wheels. A distributed team's internal communications are not the only things that require weaving. Distributed teams need to find ways to mesh what they're doing with what's going on with other teams in other parts of the organization. How can we weave together all the parts of our complex communication system so it feels like an integrated whole? What strategies can we develop so that each team member becomes part of a coherent tapestry of the team? How can we find ways to weave what we're doing into the fabric of other parts of the organization so that we are an important thread?

PARTICIPATION

What does it mean to be a full, active participant on a distributed team? In a face-to-face meeting, you can watch body language and facial expressions and many other signals to develop a sense of how people are participating—who is engaged, who has tuned out, who is angry, and who is confused. Participants in virtual teams convey this same information in different ways. It's amazing how often your impressions of what's happening can be off base because we're not used to reading the cues people give out via new media. Distributed teams need to learn how to read each other's levels and quality of participation. Participation in virtual teams needs to be very explicit. Nobody can see you nodding and giving other indications that you are there and paying attention. It's too easy for members of a distributed team to simply disappear off the radar screen of the team as a whole. Get a commitment from everyone on the team to be actively present all the time and define what that means in terms of specific actions and behaviours. For example, agree on how often the team expects to hear from everyone even when there's no specific agenda (that can be a good time for the team's conversation about future strategies). What are our mutual expectations around participation in the life of this team? What are some of the ways we will signal to each other that we are present? Listening? Confused? Reflecting? Appreciative? What does virtual head nodding look like?

FLOW

One of the key things in making a river flow is its banks . . . its container. Virtual teams can lose that feeling of flowing in a direction because their container is too weak and the energy of the team seems to leak out into the atmosphere rather than building towards something. Distributed teams also have a hard time maintaining the awareness of the whole that helps them feel like everyone is moving together. They can feel like team in a rowing shell with no idea when or how hard to pull on the oars so the shell jerks around in the water but doesn't get anywhere. It's important to facilitate a team process that heightens awareness of what is happening in all parts of the team so that the team begins to be able to sense and anticipate what's going on around the whole network of team members and can get the benefit of moving together. It's advantageous to increase and intensify team interactions early in the life of the team. One of the reasons that so many team-building processes involve games or outdoor activities is that these demand a high volume of interactions among team members in a short period that accelerates the process of being able to anticipate what each other can and will do. Using new communications media—particularly those that are not real time—can cause a team to communicate less rather than increase the interactions as needed. Teams need to develop a facilitative process that will support a higher level of engagement. Facilitation is paying attention to what is happening in your group, as distinct from what you wanted or expected would happen. It is not unlike facilitating any group: if participants aren't participating as much as you'd hoped, don't admonish them. Instead, notice what kinds of issues they are engaged in and find ways to weave those issues into your team's activity. How can we stay "in synch" with each other as a team? How will we know when the team is in the flow?"

To monetize green strategies in emerging markets therefore, there must be:

- a strong, cohesive team that will support the foundational framework mapped out within the window of opportunity,
- the integrated products
- the automated evergreen and sequential marketing strategy.

PART 2

GREEN IDEAS FOR GREENER LIVING

In this part, I am not going to start talking about the following:

- green roofs being the future of urban gardening
- natural antiseptics are safe for your skin and the environment
- natural antioxidants being the natural way to tackle ageing
- green fashion is in vogue
- ethical chocolate
- recycled arts
- greening your kitchen
- using green washing powders

All the above and more are ideal for the person that wants to start living a green life but the focus of this part is to develop an understanding of the implication of green life, green living and green lifestyle and how this impacts on our environment and on the generations unborn.

Green living is a positive lifestyle choice informed through the understanding of the impact of our behaviour on our environment and attempting to reduce our individual or society's use of the earth's natural resources to counteract the impact of resulting threats.

Let's talk a bit about Climate and its impacts. These exist in the following forms:

- unpredictable farm yields
- extinction of plants and animals
- extreme heat waves
- ozone depletion

- melting ice in arctic regions
- hurricanes
- floods and rising sea levels
- droughts

Our environment has finite resources. It is sensible to start planning on ways to maximise the use of depleting resources and find an alternative source that will ease the pressure on these resources.

Individuals can start taking positive actions to address these threats, and reduce your carbon footprint and increase the quality of your life.

I use to work for the Department of Works and Pensions (DWP) in the United Kingdom and part of my job role was to act as a Green Champion in the office. The problem was that most of the employees were not interested in green living and has no green ideas for greener living or greener lifestyle.

How do you engage people in green issues and create an enabling atmosphere for green living, green products or a green life? How can people be shown how to be eco friendly and environ mentally responsible?

The answer lies in the following:

- Creation of awareness about everything green.
- Bring issues into their world view. People associate with things that are in their world view.
- Show the link or relationship of their life with nature. They need to understand how green issues relate to them and the impact that their actions have on themselves and on the environment.
- The ecological impact of their actions should be an area of concentration.

Education about sustainability is crucial because it will enable the people to understand the link between the present and future generations. Our children and grandchildren will be able to live a quality life and be able to adequately meet their own needs if we exhibit care in the present when we are trying to meet our own needs.

I will encourage all readers to use the internet, local libraries and government agency websites to search for information on greener way of living. This will enable the process of education to be faster. All of us have a part to play.

We can decrease global warming and preserve our planet by using our knowledge and information gained on environmental care. My thinking is that if we take care of our environment, it will surely sustain us and take care of us.

Let's start from cost saving ideas:

- Reducing wastage in all forms
- Reusing items rather than discarding and buying new ones
- Use organic flowers and plants rather than artificial flowers for decorations
- Use rechargeable batteries rather than disposable ones
- Recycling old clothes rather than buying new ones
- Send email rather than sending letters
- Use refillable bottles rather than buying bottle water daily
- Turn off the tap after use in the toilets
- Power down your computers at home or work place if not in use
- Switch off lights that are not in use
- Dress up warm first rather than switch on the heater during winter
- Switch off home appliances that is not in use
- Boil only the water than you need
- Use energy efficient bulbs

The above points are not rules but ideas of things we can consciously do on a daily basis to become part of our life.

Most of the ideas given above might seem little, but they'll make a huge contribution to living green. I will quickly draw an analogy about the impact of the tiny mosquito on the life of human beings.

A bite from the mosquito will lead to malaria infection that can lead to death if not treated. The resounding impact on family and community life is tremendous.

Little actions that have great impacts are the key. The behavioural pattern needs a change. A few changes in our daily lives will surely make a huge impact on the problem of global warming.

It is a good choice to live a healthier life either by the choice of food we eat or our drink. Our actions and choices in life will have a huge impact over time, especially if it's not just a one off choice but a way of living.

Most of us behave differently at work compared to the way we live at home. We allow our employers to pay huge bills for electricity but is careful about how we use electricity at home in order to reduce our bills. It is a good choice to use resources well through management because of the overall impact of our misuse on the environment.

The government of most countries are causing more damages in dealing with challenges of nature. In the United Kingdom and some western countries the local council use salts to eliminate ice on the roadways and walkways. These salts are causing damages to the environment because of their chemical constituents.

I will mention the constituents of commercial salt below:

- Calcium chloride
- Sodium chloride
- Potassium chloride
- Magnesium chloride

These constituents are toxic to trees, plants and waterways. The salt is washed into our waters and lakes when the snow or ice melts.

It is more strategic short term to shovel the snow before it accumulate and turn into ice. De-icers must be use as a last resort and the ones use must fulfil the following conditions:

- Salt free
- Biodegradable
- Low toxicity
- Used lightly

Individuals, corporate and public sectors must embrace the use of the following:

- Green Choices
- Green Appliances
- Green Energy

The above will go a long way in saving costs and managing resources. This will definitely increase the profit margin of organisations and save on energy bills for the individual as well.

Children are the future. I believe that we must educate the future generations to start living a green life from an early age by encouraging and motivating our children to start living a greener life and embracing greener lifestyle.

The little changes that we make to our lifestyles will create a big change in the way we engage with resources.

These little changes and ways of living can:

1. save us a lot of money on the long term
2. save the environment
3. save our lives
4. save our children
5. save our country

I worked on a project in the borough of Barking and Dagenham that enabled us to facilitate the use of rockets to fasten the process of composting.

We gather household waste and use them as starting material for generating composts. The composts is later given to people that have allotments to aid the planting of vegetable and other plants.

The use of allotments and gardens to plant small vegetables should be encouraged even in the cities. This can be a source of fresh food and a sustainable way of life. The reason for this is the fact that:

*   fresh vegetables are healthier and tastier
*   they help to save resources
*   the production is a way of exercise for the planters
*   It is an engaging process that boost interest

The key reason for the development of this part is to ensure that we do not lose focus of nature. Most of the resources in the environment are finite and the more we learn how to use them to last us long the better for us.

We should start thinking how we can introduce green into every aspect of our life. This could be infused into the following:

*   The kind of car we drive
*   the kind of products we buy
*   mode of transportation
*   energy consumption
*   diet

The benefits of green living could be broadly categorised into the following:

1. Environmental
2. Economic
3. Social

It is not the intent of this book to elaborate on the above but to create an awareness of the benefit of greener lifestyle and green living.

PART 3

THE MAKING OF A MILLIONAIRE

I will like us to accept the following definition for argument sake.

A millionaire is a person whose material wealth is valued at a million dollars and can also consistently make that million dollar every year.

I am using the word in this context to refer to a person that has a cash balance of a million dollars or more, as well as other material and non-material wealth that signifies improvements in their lives that could not be quantified.

There are many people working in a job they hate just to pay their bills, while others are so tied up in self employment that they have no life.

It is very difficult to become a millionaire on paid employment. It is the dream of most people to be able to do what they want, when they want but the reality of everyday life in employment makes them realise that even the banks cannot fund their dream.

There are many bills and debts to pay. They keep pilling up for some people in a way that leads to sleepless nights because of the heavy thoughts on responsibilities.

The above case scenario impacts on the lifestyle of the majority, there seems to be no time for living life to the full.

There is a vicious cycle in living from paycheck to paycheck. The people involved seem to be perpetually in a rat race.

The importance thing that we need to recognise in the desire for money is that money in itself does not buy happiness but it brings a lot of joy for the people that we can help with the money we make.

There is a saying that the rich like the poor also cry. It seems better to cry in a limousine, if there is a need to cry at all.

The focus of the 3rd part of the book therefore is to show the reader how to become a millionaire through building an enterprise in an area of passion.

There is no need to reinvent the wheel but you can remodel it to suit your purpose.

I decided to put together an International Waste to Energy event in April 2012. The workshop fee is £1000. My intention is to raise a revenue of £1m. The event is to build an enterprise in an emerging market by monetizing green strategies.

The event will solve the problem of waste management by proffering a solution for interested parties. It will enable potential investors to see the potential in the waste management industry and learn about new technologies to manage waste. The novelty is that waste can be turned into marketable products.

By my calculation I need to sell 1000 tickets at the workshop price to make £1m but there are other ways to monetize the event as well.

Some of the other revenue generation sources for the event:

- Sponsorship income
- Income from speakers
- Income from attendees
- Ongoing residual income following the event
- Having the event paid for before it started.

I was also able to develop collaboration with other organisations across sectors. Some of the organisations are big players in the environmental and waste management sector.

I will tell you a bit of my story. The passion for care of the environment and training others to understand the purpose and benefits of caring is a fundamental part of my life. This key part has influenced my decision in life to fulfill this purpose by creating a vision of a better life. I am always eager to teach others, motivating and encouraging them to take responsibility for their own personal development. This in itself does not make the millionaire but the passion for a purpose is the key element that I want us to focus on. A person that does not stand for something will surely fall for anything.

There are many blueprints for business success. Any business process can be systemized. I think we should talk about ideas and development of opportunities first, before we delve into building, developing, growing and grooming a business into a cash cow.

There is a millionaire in every human being striving to be unleashed. This will not materialize for everybody, it is only the few that decide to go out and get their money from people's pockets that will fulfill their dream of being financially free.

The few people that are focused with passion to find a way of fulfilling their purpose in life will always find a way, if they persist or continually strive to accomplish their goal. This in itself is a vision that will give a destination that they can plan to reach with the help of the people that they can carry along.

The individual and the corporate entity should be thinking about how to maximise opportunities at this point in time.

Financing is a crucial part of any project development. The element of budgeting has to be clear. This is the reason why we need to talk a bit about finance.

Let us talk a bit about finance before we showcase the millionaire's mentality in you. I will do this by sharing the draft of a project proposal that I developed 5 years ago (2007) after deliberation with a friend on a passion to help people within the community we were living at the time. We decided to harness the potential of personal finance management skills for local benefit. My company was called Community Developers International while that of my friend was Enrich Consulting.

THE CAMPAIGN: PERSONAL FINANCE MASTERY PROGRAMME

"The problem and the need to be met involve the way that people in general relate with and use money. Effective personal finance planning and management includes the understanding of the dynamics and psychology of money; which is among the most important economic and social development resources, the lack of information and knowledge on financial literacy and discipline generally has a negative impact on the people and the future economy of a country. The project seeks to harness the potential of personal finance management skills for local benefit by firstly creating awareness about financial planning, money management, enterprise education and thereby proffering a solution through skills development.

The geographic and socio-economic factors which make it important to do something in the area are the reason for this initiative. The economic conditions and trends in the country and the region, based on research demonstrate the importance of this initiative. The need and demand for the campaign is generated by the flagrant abuse of money and the increase in debt in the United Kingdom.

The personal finance mastery and money management programme is ideal for people that are in debt and others that wants to gain personal finance management skills in general and the campaign is applicable to any area or locality in any country that wants to ensure the sustainability of her society and the proper use of these resources. Most people are not aware of how to manage money through proper planning, budgeting, forecasting, investment, building of assets and the relation to taking on additional debts. This informed the decision for the campaign. A questionnaire was collated to assess the awareness level of the people of a locality about the use of money and the result shows that less than 10% of the people are aware of the implication of their spending habits or behaviour in relation to the management of money and also cannot simply control their spending habit.

AN OVERVIEW OF THE STATE OF DEBT ISSUE IN THE UK TODAY

- The UK is presently going through a Personal Finance recession.
- The total personal debt at the end of August 2007 stood at £1,363bn.
- The rate increased to 9.9% for the previous 12 months which is equal to an increase of £115bn.
- Average consumer borrowing via credit cards, motor and retail finance deals, overdrafts and unsecured personal loans has risen to £4524 per average UK adult at the end of August 2007.
- Daily consumer borrowing is hitting £315m and more than 7,716 loan repayments are going unpaid everyday.
- The number of debt problems brought to the Citizen Advice Bureau has doubled in the last 10 years.
- Debt is now the number one issue advised on in the bureau, accounting for one in three of all enquiries and equates to 6,600 new debt problems a day. That is a staggering daily 132,000 debt problems in the UK and those are only the ones reported.

The aims and objectives of this project are to use the campaign to sensitise the people of the United Kingdom to understand the use of and the relation with money. The tools, ability and skills to get out of debt, manage their finance, stay out of debt, enhance their income, settle creditors and manage their lifestyle.

This adds to a pool of knowledge that will be useful for sustainability development and management for posterity. The preservation and enhancement of the legacy is developed from the conceptualisation of the strategies used in the research and the campaign. This will encourage communities to identify, understand, manage and appreciate money as a resource. This will increase opportunity for learning about money. All this enhances local socio-economic development, thereby enhancing people's income. We aim to provide a demonstration model of sustainable research and development as well as a money management system.

The working method used to meet our aims is to develop a research questionnaire and field assessment visits and monitoring activities using volunteers in the locality where necessary and traditional behavioural structures are studied in relation to developing regenerative perspectives on money and collating the results in order to address the problem by designing a money management system. Community Developers International has employed a financial coaching system as a tool which has been designed to address fundamental issues facing various classes of people in their personal finance. This system has imbedded in it a program called Personal Finance Mastery which can be used to totally transform the way people relate with money giving them both psychological and technical solutions to bring about positive changes in their personal finance.

Community Developers International is seeking to work with both the public and government agencies in order to support end-users who are in need of this program. Our expected outcome is that we will begin to experience a transformation from a community that is illiterate in their financial planning and undisciplined in their money management to one that can be independent and economically productive

The short and long term operation plans is to start the research in 2008, creating awareness about the campaign through the local networks like Citizen Advice Bureau, CVS Enterprise Cells, faith groups, schools, youth clubs, UK villages websites, guidebooks and through development NGOS.

The project is a pilot one that will take place between March through May of 2008; a three (3) month personal coaching on personal finance planning and money management for 36 beneficiaries across three (3) councils namely; Havering, Newham, Barking and Dagenham. The Citizens Advice Bureau (CAB) has been inundated with calls from individuals that have financial challenges that they can no longer cope with. Community Developers International has decided to provide a **free of charge** service to alleviate and address the problem of these citizens and thereby collate a report that will be useful for a full steam project that will involve more beneficiaries.

As many as twelve beneficiaries will be coached and trained each month in each of the aforementioned councils but they will have to pass through a pre-selection process to determine those that are of priority and in need of immediate assistance.

The programme will enable CDI to offer her service to more candidates after more funding has been sourced from different funding individuals or organisations.

The expected outcomes and achievements of the initiative are to create a self-sustaining project, which will be useful for posterity. We want people to understand money and its use as a solution to the problem identified by the initial research. Generate an income for the country, which will be used for social and economic development projects. CDI will produce a report charting the experience of developing and implementing the project and will use PrismCheck™; a financial coaching system as a tool and thereby organise a number of sector support activities like conferences and seminars on models for sustainable use of money and enhancing the money management functionality of the people.

The project has been process mapped to consider all the applicable details involved and place it in a controlled environment that will enable us to measure and deliver the project objectives and deliverables.

The project plan has a detailed work breakdown structure after the initial scoping and investigation has been able to identify and research the different areas.

The project approach detail how the project will be implemented and every step of the project are easily monitored.

The legacy will be preserved in resources/educational manuals and packs which will be supported by sector support activities like workshops, seminars, conferences etc that will ensure the dissemination of information, knowledge and engage the wider community in the project and the research resulting from it.

Benefits:

- This will encourage people to understand, look after and invest money and improve opportunities for learning about money.
- Open up money management resources to the widest possible audience.

- Enhance the functionality of youths through the conceptualisation of strategies.
- Increase the community Knowledge and understanding of money as a tool of preservation.
- The risks of not managing money to the wider community is mitigated

Our Proposal to the Citizen Advice Bureau (CAB)

- CDI would implore the CAB to display materials on this campaign at their advice centre
- CDI would appreciate CAB to make available the application forms to candidate that request for such
- CDI would only be able to cater for the provision of four (4) beneficiaries every month for duration of the pilot project from CAB.

The evolving opportunities will generate an income for the participating people that will be used to build and enhance an investment culture, including personal and business development.

Community Developers International has identified and committed funding to the project, contributing an initial sum of £5000, and feasibility plans have been drawn up using a prominent financial coach and director of Enrich Consulting in the United Kingdom; a leading advocate of Personal Finance planning and management strategies.

Implementation will commence in March 2008, and we are expecting to start with the CAB as one of the major channels to accessing the citizen that need the help and can benefit from this opportunity".

There is the place of passion and purpose to create an enduring vision. The lesson to be learnt is that it will be a good thing to develop and monetize strategies within your area of passion. Passion as defined by Myles Munroe is a desire that is stronger than death. It will keep you going despite all odds.

The different proposals featured in this book are therefore to help the readers see how an interest could be used to discover an individual's purpose.

This is not to discourage those that have not identified their area of passion yet. The reason for this book is to encourage readers through motivation, to identify their area of passion or see the beauty in a laudable and innovative project that could be envisioned and built into an enterprise that can be turn the individual into a business owner and the business owner into a millionaire.

Please bear with me a little bit more, before I bring out the millionaire in you. I will share two other small proposals that I wrote to the Oxford University for a Diploma in Strategy and Innovation below and part of a PhD proposal to the University of East London.

THE INFLUENCE OF STRATEGY AND INNOVATION ON GREEN CONCEPTS ASSOCIATES LIMITED'S FORAY INTO THE GLOBAL MARKET.

"My aim is to put all my business experience and knowledge into context, thereby broadening my understanding of the implication of new and emerging markets for my business. I want to find innovative solutions to the business problems and the Oxford Diploma is expected to provide the tools to do that.

I want to conceptualise a strategy that will enhance the functionality of my business and project it to the world market, boost productivity through strategic and innovative revolution.

Green Concepts specific emergent strategic, financial or organizational issues revolves around raising £50 million to expand into the international market and developing economies, providing green products and services to meet the strategic and innovation needs of developing economies and also be able to meet its objectives of building the capacity of its clientele.

There is a divergence in the effective use of innovation from the West to the developing economies. This has prompted a global shift in economic power to the developing economies. According to The Economist, The IMF forecasts that emerging economies as a whole will grow by around four percentage points more than the rich world both this year and next. If the fund is proved right, by 2013 emerging markets (on the IMF'S definition) will produce more than half of global output, measured at purchasing-power parity.

The long term success and relevance of Green Concepts as an organisation will depend on its ability to create a sustainable and effective strategic direction and gain a competitive advantage in the global and emerging markets. The analysis of key issues in strategic decision-making and process could be enhanced by the experience of the Oxford Diploma modules and also be of help in the development of the necessary tools that are needed to form a building block necessary for a good foundation.

The dynamics of new markets will place a demand on innovation strategy and the ability of Green Concepts to merge old and new evolving technologies to play a critical role in the development of underdeveloped countries by finding a synergy and a state of equilibrium between the old and the new in the provision of new products will strategically place it at the fore front of divergent economy in the global market.

The globalization and strategic module of the Oxford Diploma module states that: The appreciation of the global context is a pre-requisite for managing and leading at a strategic level in any sector. This module is designed to develop my understanding of critical trends in global business, and the factors that underlie these trends will enable the successful evaluation of the opportunities and risks of global expansion, and the tools available to implement a global strategy.

I believe that the programme is a worthwhile investment in the organisation and me. The focus on practical application will create a sustainable advantage that will develop the strength and available opportunities to counter weaknesses and threats within a SWOT analysis framework.

The implication of the principles of both competitive and corporate strategy to meet the demand of political, social and regulatory environment in which organizations operate today will enable the leveraging of available resources to meet the needs of the market".

A RESEARCH PROPOSAL
ON
THE BIODIVERSITY OF THE FLORA AND FAUNA
OF RAINHAM MARSHES: A HERITAGE PLACE

Introduction:

Rainham Marshes is one of the few ancient landscapes left in London. It is set in the industrial and urban landscape of East London and Essex. The reserve is particularly well known for its diverse birdlife and it also has one of the highest densities of water voles in United Kingdom. "Much of the original medieval land-form and marshland wildlife has been preserved and is now the largest remaining expanse of wetland bordering the upper reaches of the Thames Estuary".

Study Area:

The research will be carried out at the Rainham Marshes in the United Kingdom. The main objective of the study is the biodiversity of the area in order to determine the diverse flora and fauna life with the aim of collating a report that would be useful for information dissemination and creating awareness about the rich heritage in the community. Other related scenarios such as interview of workers, field study and use of questionnaires will also be used to collect data.

Research Objectives:

The bio-physical constraint on the earthly resources ensures that resources are finite and should be conserved accordingly to ensure sustainability.

The main objective for the research is to explore how the explicit attention to environmental modelling can be applied to determine or predict the biodiversity of the Rainham Marshes as well as determine the value of this resource and the implication of data quality on environment modelling.

The application of GIS as a tool, to digitize few selected ecosystem and process maps within the social system can be a novel conceptualising strategy.

The objectives are based on the following observations:

- The productivity paradox seems to apply in particular to support ecosystem loss during production impact on the social system.
- The finite nature of resources used for production places a bio-physical constraint on the economic system.]
- Problems of energy deficiency during waste generation could make the system less efficient
- Design of environmental models is the least supported part of the development process
- Most available support for research is aimed at the later stages (i.e. interface design), instead of the initial stages of the research (i.e. design of the plan and the interaction within the ecosystem)
- To meet the research objective, ill structured process and its content needs to get a central place in the design process which determine structure and interaction; it is this structure and interaction which in turn determine the usability of the interactive system in relation to relationships within the ecosystem.
- The question is how this attention for ill structured research can explicitly be introduced into the design process.
- The dissipation of resources in an ecosystem could be increased conservation.

Research Questions:

1. How can the biodiversity of the Rainham Marshes directly influence the interaction of the community with their heritage?
2. How can support for the heritage, traditions and culture be explicitly described during the design process without reverting to the later stages of the design?

3. How can it be ensured that these models can and will be used in a multi-disciplinary design team?
4. How can result from the analysis process be used as inputs work descriptions for resources use and appreciation of sustainability, and how the work descriptions can be used as inputs for the remainder of the research process?

Importance:

a. The research is important because of the implication for the community, the environment and the businesses and the fact that it will add information and knowledge for posterity and sector support activities which is needed for socio-economic developments.
b. The issue of bio-physical constraints facing the community in the generation of energy for the need of the world economy will be solved as finite resources are maximised
c. The anxieties over environmental damage will be reduced.

The above relates to a report by Gary Duncan, Warning as world faces $17,000bn energy bill, The Times, November 08,2005.http://business.timesonline.co.uk,which stated thus:

(". . . In a report that intensified Western pressure on oil states to boost crude output, the International Energy Agency (IEA) said that $17000billion is needed to be invested by government and companies globally by 2030 if world energy needs are to be met-$1000 billion more than estimated a year ago.

The IEA's projections showed that world energy demand is set to soar by more than 50 per cent over 25 years, raising the threat of a further surge in prices for oil and other fuels unless enough investment is made.

The report also highlighted anxieties over environmental damage from a leap in greenhouse gas emissions.

Claude Mandil, the agency's executive director, said: "These projected trends have important implications and lead to a future that is not sustainable. We must change these outcomes and get the planet on to a sustainable energy path.")

The energy need of the industry, the heavy reliance on finite resources and the need for new energy inputs make the research sufficiently broad, deep and original enough for PhD work. Other factors include the environmental challenge that confronts all industry and commerce which finds a relation with the statement by the Brundtland Commission (1987): 'There has been a growing realisation in national and international governments and multilateral institutions that it is impossible to separate economic development issues from environmental issues; many forms of development erode the environmental resources upon which they are based, and environmental degradation can undermine economic development'

Research Methodology

The need for data and computational simulations for the research makes the use of quantitative analysis methods useful. A panel research, survey and experiment will generate the data which can be analysed using various analysis techniques. The computer model and simulation of the research result will contribute to the ecosystem development which will ensure that the structure of design of the ecosystem will accommodate all the researched data inputs. This is an appropriate means of addressing the research questions. I will need to get permission to access the different records, reports and information held about the reserve in order to map the research process. The data collected will then be analysed using GIS as a means of supporting the environmental modelling of the biodiversity of Rainham Marshes after the initial selection of a sample of the whole grid.

Literature:

There is need for more information about preservation activities that support ancient landscapes in the aforementioned locality about their culture, heritage and tradition and research development on the biodiversity of the flora and fauna of Rainham Marshes; which is among the most important economic and social development resources. They will have an impact on local communities and this project seeks to harness the potentials of the biodiversity of the flora and fauna of Rainham Marshes for local benefit through the generation of more awareness about the potential of socio-economic activities and projects.

The geographic and socio-economic factors which make it important to do something in the area where the work is to be carried out is the particular location of the village which makes it a sensible place for this initiative. The economic conditions and trends in the village and the region, based on research demonstrate the importance of this initiative. The need and demand for the research is generated by the flagrant destruction of heritage places to make way for regeneration activities in the United Kingdom (BTCV, 2004).

The Rainham Marshes is one of the major remaining places that need to be conserved and held on to in order to ensure that generations to come can make use of these resources. Rainham Marshes is one of the best places for wildlife in the UK (Rainham Marshes, 2012). Everybody in the Rainham community is not aware of this rich heritage that contains a biodiversity of plants and animal life. This informed the decision for the research. A questionnaire was collated to assess the awareness level of the people of the locality about the Rainham Marshes and the result shows that less than 20% of the people are aware of the rich heritage.

The aims and objectives of this project are to use the research of the Rainham Marshes to understand the biodiversity of life at the Rainham Marshes (The Fauna and Flora of the Marshes, the different forms of animal and plant life). This adds to a pool of knowledge that will be useful for sustainability development and conservation for posterity. The preservation and enhancement of the legacy is developed from the conceptualisation of the strategies used in the research. This will encourage communities to identify, conserve and celebrate or appreciate their heritage. This will increase opportunity for learning about heritage. All this enhances local socio-economic development, thereby enhancing people's income. We aim to provide a demonstration model of sustainable research and development.

The working method used to meet our aims is to develop a research questionnaire and site visits and monitoring activities using volunteers in the locality where necessary and traditional village structures are studied in relation to develop regenerative perspectives in relation to the research to be owned and managed by the village.

The short and long term operation plans is to start the research in 2008, creating awareness about the research through the local networks like schools, youth clubs, UK villages websites, guidebooks and through development NGOS.

The expected outcomes and achievements of the initiative are to create a self-sustaining project, which will be useful for posterity. We want people to identify with and celebrate their local heritage through the research of the Rainham Marshes as a case study. Generate an income for the village, which will be used for social and economic development projects. Produce a report charting the experience of developing the project. CDI will work with RSPB to organise a number of conferences and seminars on models for sustainable research and enhancing our heritage.

The project has been process mapped to consider all the applicable details involved and place it in a controlled environment that will enable us to measure and deliver the project objectives and deliverables.

The project plan has a detailed work breakdown structure after the initial scoping and investigation has been able to identify and research the different areas.

The project approach detail how the project will be implemented and every step of the project are easily monitored.

The legacy will be preserved in resources/educational manuals and packs which will be supported by sector support activities like workshops, seminars, conferences etc that will ensure the dissemination of information, knowledge and engage the wider community in the project and the research resulting from it.

Benefits:

- This will encourage communities to identify, look after and celebrate their heritage and improve opportunities for learning about heritage.
- Open up heritage resources and sites to the widest possible audience.
- Enhance the functionality of people through the conceptualisation of strategies. Increase the community Knowledge and understanding of conservation as a tool for preservation.
- The risks of not conserving to the wider community is mitigated
- Develop socio-economic activities like tourism

We have a clear budget for the work and can justify all the expenditure. Please see attached budget and business plan.

When the funding runs out, the project will continue on a sustainable basis because of the impact of the research and the quality of the written report.

The evolving opportunities will generate an income for the village which will be used to enhance the village facilities, including personal and business development.

Community Developers International have identified and committed funding to the project, contributing an initial sum, and feasibility plans can be drawn by the research team from the University of East London; a leading advocate of traditional research technologies. As stated earlier the result of the research will be made publicly available.

This field research will encompass the environment and the community. These areas are related to my research questions in the area of instrumentation background for computational analysis, environmental modelling, data collection and solution design. Allan Brimicombe,(2003) in writing a back cover introduction for his book GIS, Environmental Modelling and Engineering was able to relate these fields when he stated the significance of modelling in managing the environment is well recognised from scientific and engineering perspectives as well as in the political arena. Environmental concerns and issue of sustainability have permeated both public and private sectors, particularly concerning the need to predict, assess and mitigate against adverse impacts that arise from continuing development and use of resources . . . and environmental modelling.

The environmental challenge, bio-physical constraints and the need for proper environmental management systems exposes the need for alternative sources of energy, materials or resources in the worldwide economic system as vividly depicted in the different workbooks of the University of Bath, (1995).Integrated Environmental Management.

Work Plan

Time-Table

This is adapted from Turpin, L. June 2005

Timed Objectives:

1st-3Th Month

a. Establishment of site(s) for data collection
b. Likely forms of data collection
c. Initial appropriate ethical relations with the participants in the study. The beginning of understandings in the major area of literature and the establishment of other areas which seems relevant. The completion of a draft introduction to the thesis, a detailed plan for the literature review and the beginning of a chapter on research procedures.

4Th-6Th Month

- Completion of the first of the twelve months of data collection, with established methodologies for doing this.
- Initial analysis, with the establishment of provisional emergent themes.
- Sufficient familiarity with literature in at least two of the above areas to provide an understanding of cogent lines of enquiry necessary to support and problematize developing findings.
- Drafts of two literature chapters, including one on research methodology.

7Th-10Th Month

- Completion of data collection.
- Familiarity with relevant area of literature.
- Completed chapter of research procedure and research methodology.
- Establishment of emergent themes and detailed plan for data analysis chapters.

11Th Month

Completed first draft of the report

12Th Month

Completed report

The three proposals above were used to depict passion and interest. They were written 5 years apart but a familiar thread of purpose and passion could be identified.

The passion for nature and green has always been the driving force in my life and this enabled me to create a vision for my purpose.

The proposals started as an idea and were developed within a window of opportunity to become an enterprise that marketed products to provide alternative sources of income.

The development of ideas is the beginning of enterprise. You will need to develop a workable plan which will be developed within a business case to convince a potential investor about the feasibility of your business.

The business or enterprise owner has a vehicle for success to make money.

OPPORTUNITY DEVELOPMENT

There is a need to actively look for opportunities in life despite the fact that opportunities are always out there, every day.

I signed a contract worth £6.5 million pounds last year by looking for opportunity in the Economist magazine that was presented in the call for a tender. Many people must have seen it and flip over that very page. The process took a period of 2 months to conclude.

The company involved was an offshore company without any representation in the United Kingdom. This is a problem for them because they could not maximize the services they are giving to their clients in the UK. I was able to fit into the equation by finding the solution that is able to create a good experience for the customer by creating an account receivable package for the client and the customers.

I was able to develop different modalities of learning for the business strategy development above to audiences through monetization strategy and product development. These are detailed below:

1. People are able to read my information through books, e-books, articles and blogs
2. People listen to my voice through audio programmes
3. They watch my videos online through Webinars, DVD
4. Seminars, speech, expositions and retreats became an avenue for information dissemination.
5. Memberships, masterminds, coaching groups and ongoing subscription were developed for special groups.

The above is just an example of how evergreen strategies are applied to situations either personal or corporate. This could be customized for individual and corporate clients.

The enterprise building and personal development process now kicks in. There are different products that could be developed from the idea above and the monetization strategy starts all over again.

The millionaire's mentality is to find a solution to a problem, build a database of potential clients that needs that solution and thereby sell the solution to the database of customers over and over again.

There are key elements of high performance supporting an analogy between the functionality of the individual, private or public sectors in relation to finding a solution to any problem.

I will talk a bit about psychology, physiology, productivity and persuasion in relation to high performance and the mentality of a millionaire that was briefly mentioned above.

PSYCHOLOGY

You have to diligently guard your mind from 'stinking thoughts' that are unproductive. Master your mind by always having it under control. Remember to continually re-programme your mindset in order not to stagnate. There are ways to improve your thought process. You should guard your minds because it's from the mind that all the issues of life come from. The kind of information you expose yourself to matters because your mind will interpret and identify with this. Your intention and initiative could become toxic as a result of stinking thoughts that fester as a result of toxic information. This will influence you and can be the determinant factor for your success or failure in life.

PHYSIOLOGY

The body is a support framework that must be taken care of. There is a need to master the body as well as the mind. The physical body should have a good stamina. There is a need to condition your body. The natural rhythm helps in energising your body and keeping it going for as long as you want. Attention should be paid to exercise, drink, food, sleep. All these help to become more alert and vibrant.

PRODUCTIVITY

There are important and urgent tasks. This is the main reason for prioritisation. In order to increase your productivity level and develop a systematic focus, all forms of distraction must be avoided. This is another mindset that will sure enhance your performance.

PERSUASION

The power of influence is crucial to high performance. To motivate or encourage others is to gain more influence with them.

I got permission from Lindsay Mckenna to use the writing below. This is to shed more light on high performance:

NINE ESSENTIAL ELEMENTS FOR HIGH PERFORMANCE

A common approach to teamwork: a robust repeatable process that can be mastered. Real benefits are derived when new teams can start up and team members can move from team to team and feel instantly "at home" with the approach being taken and the language and tools adopted. This is a great way to secure focus, speed and effectiveness.

Our consultancy support ensures that this common approach to teamwork becomes a way of life in your business, with our workshops, guidebooks and templates bringing it to life.

Engaging

The essential elements for engaging create the foundation on which high performance teams can be built. These elements are:

Purpose: The fundamental reason behind creating a Team and committing valuable business resources to support it in achieving its goals.

Commitment: A conscious decision, taken individually and collectively by the Team, to dedicate time and energy to achieve the purpose and goals set by the business.

Trust: A decision by all those involved in meeting the Team goals, to rely on each other's competence and integrity to achieve success.

Enabling

The enabling stage provides the core requirements for how the Team will operate and how individuals and Stakeholders will contribute to that operation. These core requirements are:

Capability: The skill, knowledge and capacity of the individuals, Stakeholders and Team to perform the required tasks, to the agreed timescale, to ensure the goals are achieved.

Accountability: The acceptance by all parties of the responsibilities of individuals, Stakeholders and the Team in the achievement of the Team's goals.

Principles: The agreed "rules", processes and norms which help shape and govern how the Team works together to achieve its goals. These principles provide the glue which keeps the Team together, and the necessary clarity and structure from which greater creativity, efficiency and risk-taking can emerge.

Energising

The elements of energising provide the Team with the fuel to overcome obstacles and create innovative solutions on the route to success. These elements are:

Creativity: The fostering of a team culture and environment which stimulates the creation, capture and implementation of innovative ideas.

Responsiveness: The capacity of individuals and the Team to react positively and effectively to unforeseen obstacles or changes.

Recognition: The continuous appreciation of individual and team efforts, which contribute to the building of the Team and the achievement of their goals.

HEADS: SUBHEADS:

ENGAGING:	1. Purpose.	2. Commitments.	3. Trust
ENABLING:	4. capability.	5. Accountability.	6. Principle
ENERGISING:	7. Creativity.	8. Responsiveness.	9. Recognition.

I strongly believe that the importance of high performance cannot be overstated because it is a common indicator in studying the life of millionaires. This is applicable to all readers. Please let us understand we need to improve or increase our level of performance and integrated it with the Z point.

THE Z-POINT

The Z point is that point of least resistance. It is that eureka moment, when people realises that their functionality seems to have increased. Most people could not really pin-point what they have done differently. They ponder on why things they have tried to do many times over without success suddenly appear so easy. I will not bore you with application of elements like psychology, physiology etc. I will not talk about planning nor implementation or execution of projects.

Z is the last of the alphabets. I believe that there are times when the synchronization of your mindsets becomes total; your Z point is near. There is a peak curve to your Mojo.

I believe that making a mind shift is a key indicator for success. The person that is able to function at the Z point must have the following:

- Purpose
- Passion
- Determination
- Positive thinking
- Faith
- Actions
- Focus

Everybody would like to work at the Z point. It is that strategic element of operational peak point.

The Green Millionaire is that person that has been able to merge functionalities with the Z point.

There is a strategic use of the Z point in the infusion of the concepts involved to develop a product called Z package whereby the customer or clients will be involved in a total enterprise development in order to ensure ultimate success and increase the percentage rate of success in building a green business.

THE MILLIONAIRE IN YOU

You need to dominate an area or a sector to become a millionaire. I have decided to dominate the environment and create marketable products that I can continually sell to customers to meet needs after finding a solution to perceived problems.

There is a saying about the Jack of all trade and master of none. I strongly believe that it is the expert that commands more fee than the generalist. This is the main reason why a surgeon will command more fee than generalist doctor in the field of medicine.

Every opportunity to know more about your field should be taken. People will give you more respect when you know more than them and is able to solve a particular problem.

We have deliberated on high performance in some detail above. I will suggest that any individual that wants to become a Millionaire should start a movement to become a high performer first. There are many topics or sector that could be of focus or interest. This will be the subject the individual must focus on owning within a period of one year.

I said that interest will create a desire and desire will lead to the discovery of purpose. Readers should start asking themselves the areas that they will love to dominate. The areas that they will love to learn more, excel at or talk about with passion.

This is not the only area that can bring success or enable the individual to become a Millionaire but we have discussed the place of Passion within the scheme of Purpose and Vision earlier in the book.

Readers should also start to think of what kind of products they will like to make an income from now and in the future. The short and long term planning should be a focus as well.

The book has made several attempts at sharing a set of values. Green projects have been featured to show how environmental performance could synchronise with the profit margin within a sustainability agenda. This is the storyline that has a deep connection with nature.

We have talked about different strategies that are applicable to enterprise building and green projects management. The reason for the recap is to align all the strategies with the focus of making money by developing and selling products.

The relationship between success and sanity, money and wealth, spirituality and growth could be found in a well balanced mindset.

There is a possibility for achieving success in a person that believes that it is possible and he or she can actually do it.

There is a need to develop saleable products like:

- Books
- E Books
- Audio DVD
- Video DVD
- Webcasts
- Webinars
- Tele-seminars
- Seminars
- Online Courses
- Coaching products

The reader will be thinking about the relevance of the above with the green products we have been talking about or the enterprise building.

Some of the products above are advice and training packs that can be easily produced cost effectively and can be monetized to influence people through information dissemination. This could help in increasing the database of customers for alternative products. They could be used as marketing tools as well.

The content of the context matters. The above is to break down the products into other marketable products. Imagine the rocks, digestates, gas, composts or any other products that can be developed from many processes. The strategy here is to increase the value of any of the products by ensuring that there is enough information available to a larger audience about the marketability of the products or the viability of the enterprise. This is another strategic way of thinking.

The products named above are information dissemination products that could be derived from the main products that we have mentioned earlier in the book and could increase the profit margin of customers that are thinking of being environmentally friendly.

These products that are created can then be put in a sales process via online websites. There is a need to ensure that they are of the best quality with added value and able to generate money for the seller.

We have also mentioned the place of technology in the scheme of the whole equation although I have said that it's the entrepreneur that will have to pull the strings and make the reaction a success.

The place of media is crucial within the strategic framework. The use of Face book, Twitter, Linked In, You Tube, Blogging sites and so on in an integrated format will increase online presence of the various products and get them quickly to the customers.

The above strategy will is a way of integrating social media tools into full automated marketing sequences online.

There must be a system and a structure in place to take payment quickly and cost effectively. The person that wants to become a Millionaire must be prepared and ready for the inflow of cash.

The focus at this stage is to help the reader to become confident in self and ability. Most of the steps necessary to be taken by the individual to accomplish feats are not difficult. No project can be undertaken without the determination to start.

There is a lot of systems and information in the market to help and provide support for investors. The onus is on the individual to actually engage with useable products that can aid self or business development.

Time will not permit me to talk about the importance of boldness or self-confidence, self discipline and self service. All these and more are virtues that any potential Millionaire must possess.

The lesson here is that money could be made from ever green strategies.

There is always help available in building viable enterprise in the green sector. Interested readers could access the consultancy service offered by Green Concepts Associates Limited. The details of the organisation could be found below:

Green Concepts Associates Limited
50 Cambridge Road
London IG11 8FG
Website: www.green-concepts.co.uk

You are the only barrier to your progress. If a person is able to guard the mind, the issues of life could be dealt with in a focused and systemized manner.

Now go out there and release the Green Millionaire in you.

REFERENCES

Audio English, 2012. Millionaire. [Online] Available from: http://www.audioenglish.net/dictionary/millionaire.htm. Accessed 20/02/2012

Conradin, K., Kropac, M., Spuhler, D. (Eds.) (2010): The SSWM Toolbox. Basel: seecon international gmbh. URL: http://www.sswm.info/category/implementation-tools/wastewater-treatment/hardware/site-storage-and-treatments/anaerobic-di. Accessed on 22/02/2012

Conradin, K., Kropac, M., Spuhler, D. (Eds.) (2010): *Small Scale anaerobic digester*. The SSWM Toolbox. Basel: seecon international gmbh. URL: http://www.sswm.info/category/implementation-tools/wastewater-treatment/hardware/site-storage-and-treatments/anaerobic-di. Accessed on 22/02/2012

Conradin, K., Kropac, M., Spuhler, D. (Eds.) (2010):. *Overview flow chart of small-scale agricultural biogas reactors*. The SSWM Toolbox. Basel: seecon international gmbh. URL: http://www.sswm.info/category/implementation-tools/wastewater-treatment/hardware/site-storage-and-treatments/anaerobic-di. Accessed on 22/02/2012

Conradin, K., Kropac, M., Spuhler, D. (Eds.) (2010):. *Overview flow chart of small-scale agricultural biogas reactors*. The SSWM Toolbox. Basel: seecon international gmbh. URL: http://www.sswm.info/category/implementation-tools/wastewater-treatment/hardware/site-storage-and-treatments/anaerobic-di. Accessed on 22/02/2012

Conradin, K., Kropac, M., Spuhler, D. (Eds.) (2010):. *Checking the gas valve of a floating-dome biogas reactor in India (left) and lighting the biogas flame*. The SSWM Toolbox. Basel: seecon international gmbh. URL: http://www.sswm.info/category/implementation-tools/

wastewater-treatment/hardware/site-storage-and-treatments/anaerobic-di.   Accessed   on 22/02/2012

Darryl Newport, 2008. Manufactured Research Aggregate Centre. [Online] Available from: www.uel.ac.uk/marc. Accessed 19/02/2012

Emily gems, 2012. *Green colour meaning.* [Online] Avaialble from: www.crystal-cure.com/green. html. Accessed: 22/02/2012

Green Concepts, 2012. Emerging markets. [Online] Available from: www.green-concepts.co.uk. Accessed: 19/02/2012

Greenpeace, 2012. Types of Incineration. [online] Available from http://archive.greenpeace. org/toxics/html/content/incineration/types.html. Accessed on 22/02/2012

Greenpeace, 2012. Types of Incineration. Municipal waste incinerator in Thailand. [online] Available from http://archive.greenpeace.org/toxics/html/content/incineration/types.html. Accessed on 22/02/2012

Greenpeace, 2012. Types of Incineration. Swan Hills hazardous waste incinerator. [online] Available from http://archive.greenpeace.org/toxics/html/content/incineration/types.html. Accessed on 22/02/2012

Investopedia, 2012. Dictionary. [Online] Available from: www.investopedia.com/items/ monetize.asp. Accessed 21/02/2012

Nine Essential Elements for High Performance, 2008. Lindsay McKenna Limited 2008-2010. (Online) Available from: http://www.lindsaymckennalimited.com/workshops/teams/ essential-elements.html. Accessed 22/02/2012

RSPB, 2012. Rainham Marshes. [online] Available from: http://www.rspb.org.uk/reserves/ guide/r/rainhammarshes/. Accessed 23/02/2012

RIDAN COMPOSTERS, 2009. The Ridan Composter. [Online] Available from: http://www. ridan.co.uk/. Accessed 20/02/2012

Squidoo, 2012. *Colour: Meaning, Symbolism and Psychology.* [Online] Available from: http:// www.squidoo.com/colourexpert. Accessed: 20/02/2012

Ten Key Elements for Team Leaders to Manage, 2012 (Online) Available from: http://www.scribd.com/doc/47412141/ten, www.groupjazz.com. Accessed: 20/02/2012

University of Oxford, 2012. Said Business *School*. [Online] Available from: www.sbs.oxford.edu. Accessed 20/02/2012

Wikipedia, 2012. Strategy. [Online] Available from: www.en.wikipedia.org/wiki/strategy. Accessed 22/02/2012

Wikipedia, 2012. Strategy. [Online] Available from: www.en.wikipedia.org/wiki/emerging markets. Accessed 22/02/2012